A Traveler's Guide To

CALIFORNIA BEACHES

Eric Foltz — NEWPORT BEACH PIER

AN AMERICAN TRAVELER SERIES PUBLICATION

by Elsa Ditmars

© 1994, revised 2009.

This book or any parts thereof may not be reproduced in any manner whatsoever without written permission of the publisher.

ISBN: 978-1-55838-152-0
ISBN: 1-55838-152-X

American Traveler Press
A Division of Primer Publishers
5738 North Central Avenue
Phoenix, Arizona 85012
www.AmericanTravelerPress.com
1-800-521-9921

Cover photo courtesy Judie Ajeska

10 9 8 7 6 5 4 3 2

Printed in China. Published in the United States of America

WELCOME

A seagull's view of California's 1100-mile shoreline identifies wild, rock-strewn beaches along the barren northern coast—fogbound, cold, and mysterious. Battered by powerful surf crashing against high bluffs, the beach is often littered with driftwood, logs, and mounds of seaweed. These are wonderful beaches for escape from freeway congestion, work, or sightseeing fatigue.

Winging south, the bird looks down on central coast beaches that become warm and ever more inviting to surfers, swimmers and joggers. Continuing to subtropical Los Angeles, Orange, and San Diego Counties, the edge of the sea merges into one long, usually sunbaked playground on the sand, piers, and boardwalks—the scene that lures most visitors to California.

Such contrast of climate and topography is hardly surprising on a coastal stretch equal in length to that from New Jersey to Florida. Beaches facing in every direction affect the wave action and keep the surfer's hotline buzzing. Bicyclists study patterns of wind off the sea and sand drifts on the paved bike paths. Whatever the recreation—leisurely strolling to roller blade racing—the balmy seascape is illustrated by more and more flesh exposed for tanning as the beaches approach the Mexican border.

California's coastal access and recreational facilities are subjected to the same physical forces as the shoreline itself. The width of the sandy beaches varies with the seasons as well as with the tides, and the topography of the rocky bluffs is altered by erosion. Travelers who enjoy the richness and diversity of this long coastline are advised to check, particularly after a storm, to be sure the area's facilities are accessible and usable. This is more important on the northern beaches than in the dry sunbelt south of San Francisco. Local Life Guard Stations can provide this information.

ALSO IN THE CALIFORNIA TRAVELER SERIES:

Birds of California a Guide to Viewing Distinct Vareities
Earthquake Country Traveling California's Fault Lines
Guide to Locating California Wildflowers
Parks and Monuments of California a Scenic Guide
Railroads of California Seeing the State by Rail
Whale Watching & Tidepools a Guide to Marine Life

EASY FIELD GUIDE SERIES:

Common Sea & Shore Birds of California
Invertebrate Fossils of California

CONTENTS

Welcome. 2
Beach Weather. 4
Beach Map 24

North Coast
    Del Norte 5
    Humboldt County. 7
    Mendocino County 8
    Sonoma County 10
    Marin County 11
    San Francisco Beaches 13

Central Coast
    San Mateo County. 15
    Santa Cruz County 17
    Monterey County 18
    San Luis Obispo County 20
    Santa Barbara County 21
    Ventura County 22

Southern Coast
    Los Angeles County 23
    Long Beach 29
    Orange County 30
    San Diego County 32

Popular Underwater Sites 36
Lure of the Docks & Piers 38
Pacific Flyway 43
Fair & Festival Calender 44
Beach Etiquette. 48
State Beaches. 48

Bob Yarbrough, San Diego CVB   THE SAN DIEGO COASTLINE

BEACH WEATHER

Temperatures along the California coast are more predictable than they are further inland. The moderating influence of ocean air, carried to the shore by prevailing west winds, results in a narrow seasonal range. Coastal temperatures rarely register below freezing or above 90°F. Travelers are often surprised to find that at any location on the entire 1100-mile coast, summer and winter temperatures vary no more than 10 to 20 degrees. The marine air also keeps the humidity high year round, with 65 percent humidity about normal. Contributing to this is the frequency of fog and low cloudiness common in spring and summer which usually burns off by noon.

Local topography also has an effect on the climate. Where the northern shoreline is backed by mountains, precipitation will be heavier; in the south, canyons can increase the force of the hot, dry Santa Ana winds that fuel brush fires. Some think that California's natural disasters—earthquakes, drought, floods, fires, mud slides—create a stressful environment statewide, but ever increasing population figures contradict this. The Mediterranean climate is the reason so many Californians choose not to move to more stable land.

One cause of this temperate weather is a persistent Pacific high pressure system over the ocean. Currents, ocean floor contours and depths, wind speeds, and exposures all affect water temperatures. This explains the contrast between the cold waters off San Francisco and the warmer swimming on south-facing beaches like **Santa Cruz, Santa Barbara, Malibu** and **Long Beach**.

NORTH COAST

DRIFTWOOD ON THE NORTH COAST

DEL NORTE COUNTY

Del Norte, the state's northernmost county, meets the sea with stretches of sand indented by coves often hidden beneath looming rocky cliffs. Sculpted into dunes and caves by fierce storms and high tides, these beaches are littered with shells, driftwood, and seaweed. Here is a beachcomber's dream of rocks, pebbles, fossils and the hardiest tidepool creatures. Crabs, abalone, clams and burrowing mollusks thrive along these chilly, fogbound shores.

Marine air averages from 47°F. in January to 57°F. in August. Crescent City receives an average of 75 inches of rain annually compared to San Francisco's 20 inches and San Diego's 12 inches. Battered by wind and rain, this coastal zone is altered daily and bears no resemblance to the sunbather's beaches of the Southern California, where temperatures range between 65 and 75°F. year round.

Farthest north, nearly on the Oregon border, is **Pelican State Beach**, a small, secluded getaway just off Highway 101. About 20 miles south is Crescent City, home to the Yurok and Tolowa Indians until 1850, when prospectors settled the city and developed its port for the transfer of gold from southern Oregon strikes and those of the nearby Smith River watershed. All of **Crescent Beach** was once staked for gold. By 1870, gold fever had subsided and lumber became the north country's major export. Fortunately, unrestricted cutting of the majestic, centuries-old redwoods has been curtailed.

Visitors seek out this shore to enjoy solitude, jogging, beach walks, fishing, or the awesome redwood forests.

Redwood National Park — COASTLINE

Crescent Beach has picnic tables in a grassy area between the parking lot and beach.

On the seaward side of a small islet, 250 yards west of the breakwater, the Battery Point Lighthouse guides mariners safely into **Crescent Bay**. Built in 1856, this white-painted Cape Cod-style dwelling with brick tower is typical of the first 16 west coast lighthouses designed by Washington, D.C. architects. These stand in sharp contrast to the Spanish Revival influence on lighthouse construction that became popular in the 1920s. Now open as a museum and accessible only at low tide, visitors walk across the sandy isthmus for tours. The lighthouse. it is open to the public April through September. The Del Norte County Historical Society supports this facility as well as the nearby Crescent City Museum.

South of Crescent City is **Del Norte Coast Redwoods State Park** swimming is not advised but the area has excellent tidepools. Then 25 miles south of Crescent City are **Redwood National Park** and **Prairie Creek Redwoods State Park** cooperatively managed by the National Park Service and the California Department of Parks and Recreation. The National Park encompasses 110,000 acres of redwood trees, beaches, and rain forests. The area offers camping and a trail system leading both inland and along the coast. The Newton B. Drury Scenic Parkway off Highway 101 is the access to Prairie Creek. The 10-mile long Gold Bluffs Beach has a campground but is not accessible to vehicles pilling trailers.

NORTH COAST

Eureka/Humboldt Co. CVB TRINIDAD BAY

HUMBOLDT COUNTY

Home to the spectacular ancient coastal Redwoods, Humboldt County offers a 110-mile coastline of beautiful vistas and beaches. **Patrick's Point State Park** covers 632 acres of forests, blufftop meadows on rocky headlands, and a sandy beach. At the park are campsites, picnic areas and a campfire center. The Rim Trail follows an Indian route along the bluffs for two miles. At the Visitors Center is a small natural history museum and an Indian village reconstruction. Birds are abundant, and migrating gray whales can be seen from the bluffs. Adjacent **Agate Beach** attracts collectors of small pieces of agate and jade, where sea lions bark off shore.

Heading south, a long spit separates Arcata Bay from the ocean. The sandy beach can be reached by walking over the dunes from several parking areas off Route 255. **Trinidad State Beach** and harbor area, **Little River State Beach** and **Mad River Ocean Beach** provide good ocean access, with parking and picnic areas. The walk around **Trinidad Head** is one of the most scenic in the state. Begin at the beach area below the head and follow signs for the Tsurai Trail.

Eureka lies on **Humboldt Bay**, second largest enclosed bay in the state. Gold strikes on the Trinity River brought Europeans to the Humboldt coast in 1850, and the port towns of Trinidad, Arcata, and Eureka vied for dominance. The timber industry, commercial fishing, and tourism support the region today.

NORTH COAST

Fort Bragg-Mendocino C of C FORT BRAGG—MENDOCINO COAST

MENDOCINO COUNTY

Although the U.S. government now limits salmon fishing because of seriously depleted runs, and also curtails the timber industry, this region has found a new economic base. Its resource is the scenic splendor of California's 300-mile northern coast, from the Oregon border to San Francisco. Mendocino County's 90-mile shoreline is dotted with picturesque lumber towns and old ports. Country inns, imaginative restaurants, and galleries attest to Mendocino's modern image as an artists' haven. Travelers enjoy spectacular seascapes driving the oceanfront highway and are drawn to the quaint 19th-century clapboard houses built by New England pioneers who settled the area. Across the road are the magnificent headlands of **Mendocino Headlands State Park**, overlooking **Mendocino Bay** with **Big River Beach** below.

Lonely shores that once supported hunting and fishing for isolated tribes of native Americans now cater to travelers seeking a wilderness experience. Urbanites don sou'westers to walk remote beaches, cowboy boots and waterproof woolens to gallop along **Ten Mile Beach**, longjohns under hightop waders to cast into icy breakers.

Dramatically eroded sea cliffs protect Mendocino County's pocket beaches from winds that elsewhere produce giant surf and carve rocky terraces. Occasional deep ravines of stream, creek, and river inlets cut the terraces. The shoreline is characterized by "sea stacks," towering

FORT BRAGG—MENDOCINO AREA

rock outcroppings just off shore, adjacent to rugged promontories that thrust into the ocean. Such breathtaking scenery challenges drivers on Highway 1—a beautiful, crooked road of blind turns, sharp hills, and delicate bridges. The route winds through untouched open land where cattle graze between dark rich forests of spruce, hemlock, redwood and pine.

Park headquarters at **Jughandle State Natural Reserve** has brochures for self-guided ecological tours. Five miles of nature trails traverse the headlands and coastal terraces to a sandy beach at the mouth of Jughandle Creek. **Sinkyone Wilderness State Park** consists of 7,312 acres of undeveloped beaches, bluffs, and dense redwood forests from King Range to Bear Harbor. Heading south between Sinkyone and **Manchester State Beach** is a smaller beach, popular for fishing and hiking: **Westport-Union Landing State Beach**.

Manchester State Beach, measuring 1400 acres, is one of the county's largest. Offshore is a popular underwater park for diving. Just east of the beach is a privately owned campground with store, gameroom, swimming pool, hot tub, and showers. Nearby Point Arena Lighthouse, built in 1870, has one of the most powerful lights on the coast. It is open daily for tours, and three former lighthouse keepers' cottages are available for rent. The rocky, driftwood-strewn **Arena Cove Beach** has a 322-ft.-long wheelchair accessible steel pier. Boat launch and hoist are available all year with fish-cleaning tables, outdoor showers and offshore moorings.

NORTH COAST

Liz England, Sonoma CO. CVB — BODEGA BAY

SONOMA COUNTY

Best known for its verdant valleys of grapes, famous wineries, and beckoning country inns, Sonoma County has a lesser known but equally interesting shoreline. Historic Fort Ross sits on a coastal bluff 8 miles north of the Russian River estuary. Occupied from 1812 to 1841 by the Russian American Fur Company, the fort as a base for seal and otter hunting. The Russian River, popular in spring and summer for canoeing and swimming, flows into the Pacific at Goat Rock in Sonoma Coast State Park. Goat Rock Beach is home to a colony of harbor seals that draw travelers year round.

The southern third of this coast, the **Sonoma Coast State Beach**, includes more than a dozen sandy coves, acres of dunes, and secluded pocket beaches between Goat Rock and Bodega Bay. Though a favorite beach for fishing, high surf and strong rips make walking even in shallow water dangerous. No swimming is advised on Sonoma Coast beaches.

Bodega Bay is crowded during salmon season and a Fisherman's Festival is held here in April. Sportfishing excursions depart from Sonoma County docks or Porto Bodega. The University of California's Bodega Bay Marine Laboratory, a research and aquaculture facility, offers guided tours and is open to the public on a limited basis.

———————— NORTH COAST ————————

Larry Ulrich, CA Office of Tourism — POINT REYES LIGHTHOUSE

MARIN COUNTY

One of the seven designated national seashores in the U.S., the 64,000-acre **Point Reyes Peninsula** is the most striking feature of this northern county. Frequent fogs, steep headlands, forested ravines, wild winds and waves have racked up a long history of shipwrecks on this peninsula, which lies between the ocean and the notorious San Andreas Fault. To help ships navigate these treacherous shores, two lighthouses were built in the 1800s: Point Bonito and Point Reyes. Both are open to the public and are now prime lookouts for migrating gray whales.

First to settle Point Reyes were the Miwok Indians who inhabited more than 100 villages on the peninsula when English explorer Francis Drake supposedly landed in 1579. Spanish missionaries arrived in 1820. Their settlements resulted in confiscation of land and introduction of European diseases, which eventually led to the destruction of the Miwok culture.

One of the few full-time ornithological stations in the U.S., the Point Reyes Bird Observatory's Palomarin Field Station is located at the southern end of the **Point Reyes National Seashore**. Their Marine Ecology Division is a leader in seabird and marine life research. The Visitor Center is open year round.

Just across the bridge from San Francisco, the **Golden Gate National Recreation Area** attracts city dwellers and tourists to the grassy bluffs and sandy beaches of **Marin Headlands**. Once an army post, this park of parade grounds, officers quarters, decaying bunkers, barracks, and

Betsy Ditmars   CHRISSY FIELD BEACH, NEAR THE GOLDEN GATE

an old balloon hangar, now houses a hostel and campgrounds within sound of the Golden Gate Bridge foghorn.

Favorites on this long seashore are **Stinson, Red Rock, Muir**, and **Rodeo** beaches. Stinson, the choice of advanced surfers, is patrolled by lifeguards in the summer. Facilities include a picnic area, snack bar, and wheelchair-accessible restrooms. No pets are allowed on the beach. Part of **Mount Tamalpais State Park**, Red Rock is reached by a steep trail down to a small beach that can attract nude bathers. Muir Beach is known for fishing, picnicking and, in winter, the blankets of monarch butterflies draped over nearby pine trees.

The pebbly Rodeo Beach, between the ocean and **Rodeo Lagoon**, is a habitat for several uncommon species of fish and birds, including the California brown pelican. Former army bunkers house environmental, educational, and interpretive programs like the California Marine Mammals Center and the Marin Headlands Institute. Accessible by a steep ½ mile walk the **Point Bonita Lighthouse** offers spectacular ocean views.

Kurt Molnar   EXCURSION TO ALCATRAZ

SAN FRANCISCO BEACHES

The trails that lead to **Baker Beach** offer wonderful views of the Golden Gate Bridge and Marin Headlands. The northern end of the beach is popular with nude sunbathers. **China Beach** is San Francisco's only ocean beach safe for swimming. This small crescent is protected from the rip currents and huge waves of the other beaches. Inside the Bay, **Alcatraz Island** and **Angel Island** have beach picnic areas and some camping. A panorama of commercial vessels, harbor ferries, cruise ships, and colorful sailing and windsurfer races makes these superb sightseeing locations.

Twenty miles offshore from the Golden Gate lie the **Farallon Islands**. Beaches on these remote islands are reached by excursion boats and are of interest primarily to bird watchers, since they are important breeding grounds for pelicans, storm-petrels, and murres. In the 1850s the Farallon Egg Company was established to supply murre eggs for the booming population of San Francisco. The practice of robbing these island nests was banned when the seabird count declined dramatically.

Twice each day, the 400 square miles of **San Francisco Bay** drain and fill through the Golden Gate Bridge, generating tremendous coastside currents along the beaches. From a heaving gray ocean, breakers tear at the base of the rock promontory that supports the southern tower of the great bridge. Intrepid surfers look hungrily at the giant waves hurled around the bridge's base—a world of furious white water to "punch through" with their big boards. Then, from the smooth surface of a swell, they wait for that special

Betsy Ditmars — SURFING UNDER GOLDEN GATE BRIDGE

wave. Of the estimated 5 million surfers worldwide, 1½ million live on the west coast of the United States, but only the most skilled surf in San Francisco.

At **Fort Point**, a few miles west by bike or car from San Francisco's famous Fisherman's Wharf, travelers can visit the interior of an 1853 brick fortress, now a National Historic Site with museum and bookstore. Park rangers in Civil War costumes conduct tours through the fort.

Ocean Beach's four miles of coastline is a good flat beach for an exhilirating hike, but year-round wind and fog discourage picnics or sunbathing. Three miles west of downtown, it is a surfer heaven. At dawn they shiver on the beach gauging wave intervals, direction of the swells, the force of tremendous tidal currents and listening on van radios to meteorological reports from hundreds of miles out at sea.

Offshore winds make January the best month for "big, clean waves," larger, more concave, and faster. This treacherous seashore is not for beginners, who should learn at Santa Cruz or areas farther south. Water temperatures range from the high 40s to mid-50s and the air can be below freezing. To avoid hypothermia, surfers wear full-length wetsuits, booties and gloves. Even so, after two hours in the icy waters, hands become numb and headaches intense.

CENTRAL COAST

Jim Bohannan PIGEON POINT LIGHTHOUSE

SAN MATEO COUNTY

The Central Coast stretches 350 miles from San Francisco to Ventura and includes some of California's best beaches, coves, and forested blufftops between spectacular sea cliffs. Fifty-five miles of this Pacific coastline lie in San Mateo County with beaches accessible to populated urban areas like San Jose, San Francisco, and Daly City. Too cold and hazardous for swimming, they attract people for pier and shore fishing, tidepooling, marine mammal watching and picnicking. At **Año Nuevo State Natural Reserve**, visitors snap close-up photos of elephant seals that come ashore to breed. These large pinnipeds reach lengths of 14 feet and weigh up to three tons. Permits are required to access the seal viewing areas. Restrooms, drinking water and picnic tables are available near the Visitor Center which offers Natural History exhibits. Pets are not allowed in the reserve.

Rich soils of the marine terraces high above the beach support coastal agriculture. **Half Moon Bay** is renowned for its fields of autumn pumpkins, Christmas trees, and artichokes. The same heavy fogs that sustain the harvests have contributed to numerous shipwrecks throughout the county's history. Pigeon Point lighthouse perches 100 feet above the rocky point where the Boston clipper ship *Carrier Pigeon* broke up on these shoals in 1853. In 1960 the Coast Guard built four bungalows as keepers' dwellings, which are now subleased as Hostels. Overnight visitors can tour the 115-ft.-high circular brick tower and see its great

San Mateo Co. CVB — ELEPHANT SEAL

first-order Fresnel lens, lighting sea lanes 25 miles into the Pacific. When, in 1896, the freighter *Columbia* ran aground off Año Nuevo, Pescadero's residents salvaged its cargo of white paint, used it liberally on the town's buildings, and have since maintained the tradition of painting their houses white. A vista point overlooks **Pescadero State Beach** and the **Pescadero Marsh**.

OTHER AREA BEACHES:

Pacifica State Beach, *Wide crescent shaped beach operated by City of Pacifica. Preferred by surfers, but hazardous due to rip currents.*

Gray Whale Cove State Beach, *A sheltered cove surrounded by cliffs that drop abruptly. Clothing is optional.*

Montara State Beach, *Popular location to explore tide pools, Hostel at Montara Lighthouse has bike rentals and day-use facilities.*

Half Moon Bay State Beach, *Four miles of sandy beach ideal for sunbathing, fishing and picknicking.*

San Gregorio State Beach, *There is a driftwood-strewn estuary and a freshwater marsh at the back of this wide sandy beach.*

Pomponio State Beach, *Miles of gently sloping, sandy beaches with roaring surf. There are picnic tables overlooking the ocean and day-use cooking grills.*

Bean Hollow State Beach, *Swimming is dangerous but the fishing, picknicking and beachcombing are excellent. Marine life in the tidepools is abundant.*

CENTRAL COAST

SANTA CRUZ COUNTY

Along Santa Cruz County's 42 miles of coastline, mountains shelter the coastal terraces that produce acres of brussels sprouts, lettuce, artichokes, and flowers. The city of Santa Cruz, founded by Father Fermin Francisco de Lasuen in 1791, is a tourist mecca with a mile-long protected beach, warm water swimming and body surfing, and the famous boardwalk amusement park—the last of its kind still operating on the Pacific Coast. The city provides beach access by ten stairways found on blufftop streets.

Capitola City Beach, located seaward of the city esplanade; has kite flying, volleyball, and warm swimming water.

Seacliff State Beach This 85-acre beach is a popular swimming spot. The visitor center has a large covered picnic area. and fishing pier leading to a scuttled 435-foot long concrete supply ship, the Palo Alto, built during World War I. The ship once hosted entertainment venues but has become unsafe and is closed to the public. The pier, however, continues to be a favorite fishing spot.

OTHER AREA BEACHES:

Natural Bridges State Beach The natural bridge offers a vantage point for observing migrating whales, otters, seals and shore birds with sandy beach and tidepools below. Eucalyptus-shaded picnic grounds are located near Moore Creek which flows to the ocean.

Lighthouse Field State Beach. Also known as Point Santa Cruz. Birds, surfers, tourists, sea lions and wintering Monarch Butterflies are drawn here. The Mark Abbott Memorial Lighthouse at Point Santa Cruz overlooks Monterey Bay and the Pacific Ocean. The Lighthouse overlooks legendary surfing spot Steamer Lane and houses the Santa Cruz Surfing Museum.

Twin Lakes State Beach, 28 acres extends by bike/pedestrian path on both sides of Santa Cruz Small Boat Harbor. Facilities include volleyball nets and standards, fire rings, jetty fishing.

New Brighton State Beach, has 115 campsites on 68 acres with view of Monterey Bay. Beach access via a stairway from parking lot or driveway to the edge of the sand. Capitola Village free shuttle operates in summer to New Brighton Beach. Surf fishing and clamming.

Manresa State Beach is reached by a stairway and path down the bluff from the main parking lot or via a paved accessway off San Dollar Drive. High surf and rip currents lure more sightseers than swimmers.

Sunset State Beach, has 7 miles of beachfront; 90 campsites and a picnic area. In the spring, multicolored poppies and blue lupine bloom in the meadows.

Palm State Beach, Watsonville. Fishing, swimming and long walks on the wide beach are popular activities. Picnic tables are available.

CENTRAL COAST

Martin Brown, Montery VCB   MONTEREY BAY

MONTEREY COUNTY

Monterey Bay was sighted in 1542 by explorer Juan Rodriguez Cabrillo. Today its coastline is world famous, the most photographed scene probably the Big Sur Coast, with its windswept cedars clinging to cliffs 800 feet above the crashing surf. **Monterey Peninsula**, at the southwest end of the bay, offers a superb 17-mile coastal drive along a toll-gated road that winds through Del Monte Forest. Along the route are pocket beaches and surfing areas. This area is home to Steinbeck's Cannery Row and the Monterey Bay Aquarium.

In north Monterey County, **Zmudowski State Beach** features the Pajaro River estuary. This 177-acre beach is popular for surfing and fishing. Horses are permitted near the waterline except in summer.

Boardwalk and steep dune trails lead to the 246-acre **Salinas River State Beach**, a sandy beach popular for fishing, clamming, hiking, and horseback riding. The Salinas River Wildlife Area's 518-acre refuge is just south of the beach. Close by is **Marina State Beach**, accessed by a 2,000-ft. boardwalk, with an observation platform at the halfway point. Kite-flying and picnics are popular here. Swimming is unsafe due to strong currents, but there is a hang-gliding deck with launch ramp at the central part of the beach.

Asilomar State Beach and Conference Grounds in Pacific Grove offers visitors an assortment of rocky shores with tidepools, dunes, and sandy beach areas. There is a diving area, but no swimming because of hazardous rip currents. The conference center, in a wooded landscaped setting, has meeting space and lodging.

Many consider **Carmel** the jewel of the Monterey County coast. On this clean, white sandy beach one is likely

Elsa Ditmars   MONTEREY BAY KAYAK

to see an artist's easel, paints and picnic basket stowed beneath evergreen branches of cypress or pine. The village is quaint; its shops, cozy inns, and cafes offer ideal posing for tourist cameras.

Point Lobos State Natural Reserve comprises 1,276 acres of headlands with spectacular coastal views, sandy coves and beaches, tidepools, and Monterey cypress groves. More than 300 plants and 250 bird and animal species inhabit the trails and picnic areas. Swimming is allowed in China Cove. There are guided tours in summer; the interpretive center has a small museum with artifacts from whaling days. Sea lions on offshore rocks and floating sea otters can be seen from bluffs.

Pfeiffer Beach, its beautiful white sand dramatically backed by steep cliffs, sea stacks and sea caves, is reached by a trail from the parking lot one mile south of **Pfeiffer-Big Sur State Park** entrance. Giant waves crash through natural rock arches, and Sycamore Creek empties onto the beach in a small lagoon.

OTHER AREA BEACHES:

Moss Landing State Beach, also known as ***Jetty Beach***, *is on the border with San Mateo County., 55 acres, windsurfing, birdwatching and picnics.*

Monterey State Beach *is comprised of three separate beaches approximately a mile apart. Take your pick: swimming, picnicing, beachcombing, surfing, tidepool watching, scuba diving, kayaking, kite-flying, volleyball.*

Carmel River State Beach, *popular for scuba diving the surf can be hazardous, also known as San Jose Creek Beach. There is a marsh at the north end and a lagoon at the mouth of the Carmel River. Undersea Carmel Bay Ecological Reserve is adjacent to the beach.*

CENTRAL COAST

San Luis Obispo Co. VCB — MORRO ROCK

SAN LUIS OBISPO COUNTY

This 96-mile-long coastline has sandy beaches, sheltered bays, and agricultural land west of the Santa Lucia Mountains. Morro Rock is the tallest of 8 volcanic peaks between **Morro Bay** and San Luis Obispo. The county's northern coast has miles of near-empty beaches. At turn-outs along Highway 1, travelers can watch the sea crash onto craggy cliffs and sandy coves.

Pismo Beach—23 miles of beach and windswept sand dunes—is California's only "driveable" beach. Horses or off-road vehicles can be taken onto 6 miles of sand. Travelers can hike the dunes to Oso Flaco Lake or dig for Pismo clams. Legend says that 150,000 people once removed 75,000 pounds of clams during a single weekend at Pismo Beach. Now clamming is strictly regulated: clams must be at least 4-1/2 inches and only 10 may be taken at a time.

William Randolph Hearst Memorial State Beach offers excellent swimming, protected from heavy surf and wind by San Simeon Point. Along the 1,000-foot pier are boat charters and fishing equipment rentals. There are picnic tables in eucalyptus groves just north of the pier. Nearby is Hearst Castle, 120 acres of hilltop gardens and herds of exotic animals.

OTHER AREA BEACHES:

Cayucos State Beach, popular fishing pier is lit at night and wheelchair-accessible. BBQ and picnic facilities near Cayucos Vets Hall.

Morro Strand State Beach, Just north of Morro Bay. A 3 mile strand of beach with an entrance at both ends. Fishing, jogging, kite-flying and windsurfing are popular.

Montaña de Oro State Park, 8,400 acres with campgrounds and three miles of coastline. Bluff top trails, sandy beaches and rocky pocket beaches.

Avila Beach, children's playground, fishing pier, showers, fish-cleaning facilities. Lifeguards spring and summer.

CENTRAL COAST

Elsa Ditmars — ARCH ROCK, ANACAPA ISLAND, CHANNEL ISLANDS

SANTA BARBARA COUNTY

The city of Santa Barbara is a showcase of Spanish and mission-style architecture. Its adjacent coastline stretches along 8 miles of wide, gently curving beaches fringed with palm trees. A bike path winds the length of the strand, past shaded picnic tables, historic **Stearns Wharf**, a picturesque breakwater-protected yacht harbor, and beachside art exhibits.

Goleta Beach County Park, east of the University of California Santa Barbara (UCSB) campus, with grassy picnic areas. Services include a fishing pier with boat hoist, children's playground, volleyball courts, restaurant, and snack shop. Canoeing and bird watching attract travelers to the 350-acre **Goleta Slough** wetland.

Across the Santa Barbara Channel lie four of California's eight **Channel Islands**. To explore the rare flora and fauna of these island wildernesses, excursions run daily from the Santa Barbara pier and Ventura's marina to the south. Just south of Santa Barbara is **Carpinteria State Beach**, known as the safest beach on the coast because the shallow off-shore shelf prevents rip currents; there are summmer lifeguards. A Chumash Indian Interpretive Center is here, along with campsites and a grassy picnic area. A popular stretch of surfing beach is dubbed "the tarpits."

OTHER AREA BEACHES

Gaviota State Park, 2,776-acres includes 5.5 miles of shoreline, a picnic area, campground and fishing pier; lifeguards in summer.

Refugio State Beach, foot of Refugio Road.; sandy beach with rocky coves, tidepool habitats, 85 campsites, connected by bike trail with El Capitan State Beach.

El Capitan State Beach, hiking trail leads to grassy picnic area along rocky shoreline, campsites by reservation. El Capitan Point popular for surfing.

CENTRAL COAST

Ventura CVB   VENTURA HARBOR

VENTURA COUNTY

On the map, Ventura County's beaches face west or south. Waves that break on west-facing **Oil Piers Beach** please surfers, who in turn put on a good show for beach-going spectators. Surf action is usually gentler on the south-facing beaches like **Sycamore Cove Beach** near the Los Angeles County line. The wheelchair-accessible facilities here include a wooden walkway that leads out to the sandy beach from grassy picnic areas with tables and cooking grills. There are lifeguards in summer. Sycamore Cove Beach is part of **Point Mugu State Park** that encompasses 5 miles of ocean shoreline and 70 miles of hiking trails

McGrath State Beach, 295 acres includes dunes, sandy beach, campground, and a nature trail leading to the Santa Clara Estuary Natural Preserve, a marsh area wildlife sanctuary that is one of the California coast's best bird-watching areas.

Port Hueneme's beach park is a broad sandy strand equipped with playground facilities, protected picnic sites, a grassy area and a snack bar. A pedestrian/bike path runs along the beach to the port's 1,240-foot-long, T-shaped fishing pier. Open 24 hours, the lighted pier has cutting tables with sinks, a bait shop and cafe.

OTHER AREA BEACHES:

Emma Wood State Beach popular for swimming, surfing and fishing. Ventura River estuary at the southeast end of the park attracts a wide variety of wildlife.

San Buenaventura State Beach, a wide, sandy beach protected by breakwaters; good swimming where lifeguards are on duty. Picnic areas, snack bar, beach equipment rentals, volleyball, outdoor showers, dressing rooms. 1,700-foot-long Ventura Pier has restaurant, snack and bait shop.

SOUTHERN COAST

Michele & Tom Grimm, LA CVB   VENICE BEACH BOY

LOS ANGELES COUNTY

Every year, millions of travelers visit the 76 miles of coastline that make up Los Angeles County's western boundary. Tourism is especially high in summer when the ocean warms up to 70° F. Summer midday temperatures average in the 70s and 80s after the usual early morning fog burns off.

Leo Carrillo State Park, a 3,000-acre park at the west end of Malibu, offers good surfing, swimming, diving, sea caves, tide pool exploration, hiking trails and camping. **Staircase Beach**, the northernmost developed portion of Leo Carrillo Beach, is accessible from a path at the state beach parking lot on the Pacific Coast Highway. There is additional access from North Beach Campground.

The south-facing **Zuma Beach**, just west of **Point Dume**, is Los Angeles' largest county-owned beach. The swimming here is excellent, there is also a tots' playground, volleyball courts and food stalls. Southeast from neighboring Point Dume, the mountains drop sharply into **Santa Monica Bay**, resulting in a series of rocky coves, headlands, jagged points and small pocket beaches. This rural coastline faces south and is a mecca for serious surfers looking for variety in currents and waves. It is also the top choice for celebrities seeking warmth and privacy in luxurious walled beach houses of the Malibu area.

Will Rogers State Beach has been the host of many movies and television shows. This beach is popular for swimming, diving, and surfing.

(continued on page 26)

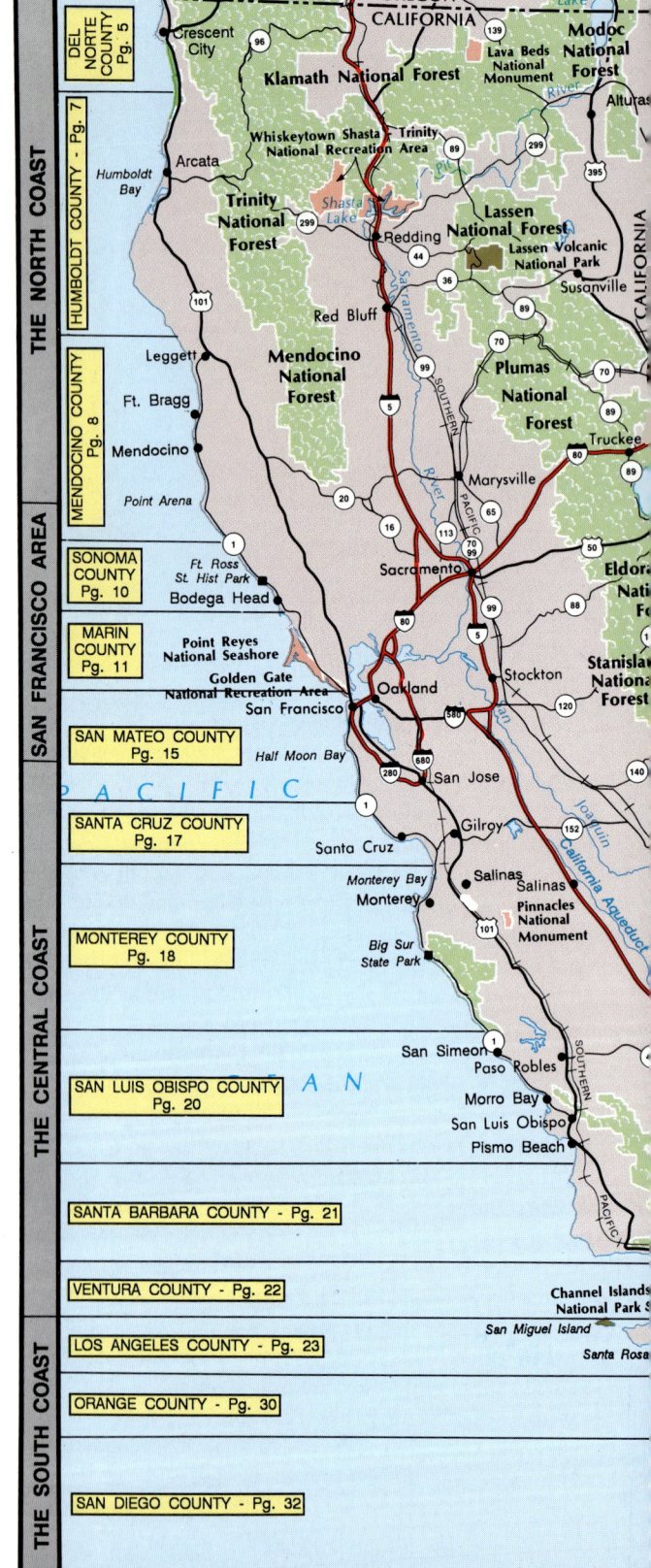

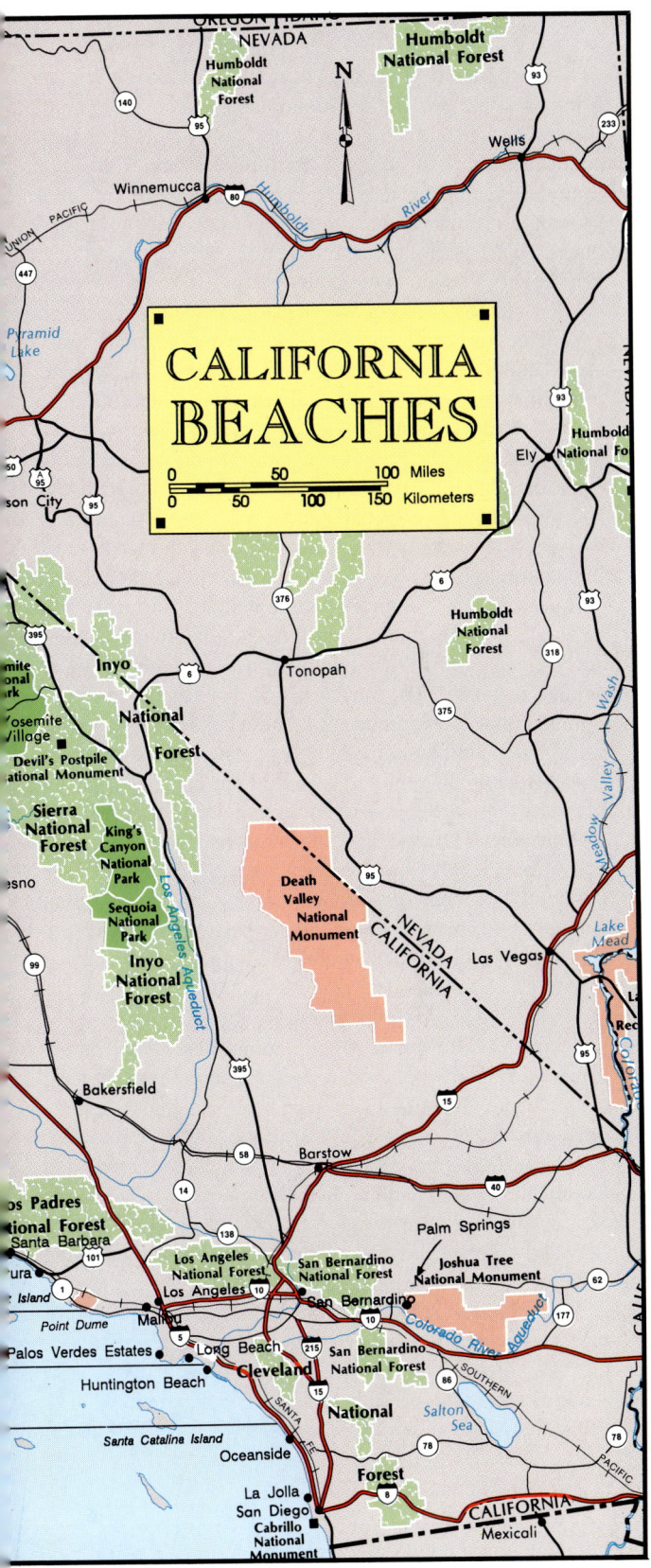

Santa Monica State Beach and **Venice Beach** are the prime destinations for sightseers, sunbathers, swimmers, surfers, and fishermen. The South Bay bicycle trail runs south from here 20 miles to **Redondo Beach**. Wide and sandy, these popular playgrounds are highlighted by Santa Monica's renowned pier with its historic carrousel, frequently used by Hollywood studios as a setting for movies. Restaurants, street merchants, shops, and amusement arcades glamorize Santa Monica and Venice beaches—the "in" place for people watching. Hollywood hopefuls, sideshow and athletic performers hang out here. Boating and pier fishing are available as well as rentals of all kinds.

Dockweiler State Beach, an extremely wide, sandy beach just west of the Los Angeles Airport, is accessible from the Pacific Coast Highway at Imperial Highway. Facilities include volleyball courts, snack bar, a picnic area with firepits, an RV park, outdoor showers and wheelchair ramps from blufftop to beach bike path. The seashore cities of Los Angeles' South Bay—Manhattan, Hermosa, and Redondo— are connected by a stretch of broad beaches, accented by fishing/entertainment piers and marinas (For details, see page 40). Surf festivals, sandcastle and kite-flying contests, fishing derbies, volleyball tourneys, skateboarding, rollerblades and biking draw people to these playgrounds year-round. They are kept clean, served by lifeguards and are spacious enough to accommodate holiday crowds. The best time to swim and bodysurf these oceanfronts is July through October when the water reaches 68° to 70° F. **Torrance Beach**, between Redondo Beach and the small curve of **Palos Verdes Beach**, has wide ramp access from a blufftop, as well as a lifeguard, showers, and bike path.

Offshore 22 miles and accessible by excursion boat or helicopter is **Catalina Island**, the choice of weekend or day trippers. Boat owners from Los Angeles' and Orange County's crowded marinas escape here from office, factory or freeway. Daily sailings bring vacationers from Redondo Beach, Los Angeles Harbor, Long Beach, Newport, and Oceanside. They disembark in the tiny port town of Avalon. Set against steep scrub oak and chaparral-covered hills, flowered balconies, red-tiled roofs, and terrace dining, the ambiance is purely Mediterranean.

The island's 76 square miles is 86 percent nature preserve. Small vans take visitors over rough terrain to see buffalo, wild boar, rabbits, and sheep in the canyons with seabirds soaring overhead. Naturalists come here to study the many unique endemic plants and trees. Seals bark in the coves, and glassbottom boats let sightseers observe the marine life habitats along the shore.

Cabrillo Marine Aquarium   SAND SCULPTURE, SAN PEDRO SEA FAIR

Secluded arcs of sandy beaches are almost hidden by the high-cliffed shoreline of this volcanic island. Many travelers never venture out of Avalon with its crowded little crescent beach, souvenir shops, inns and restaurants. But those with more time head for the hills and the lovely sandy coves on the Catalina Channel shore or, on the windward side, **Little Harbor** and **Ben Weston** beaches, one-time Chumash Indian settlements. Camping is allowed with reservations, skin and scuba diving with licenses. Rentals and air refills are available at Two Harbors and Avalon. Pets are not permitted.

Palos Verdes Peninsula's rocky shore is best seen from blufftop walks and scenic overlooks. Surfers have beaten precipitous foot paths down to the beach, but these are extremely hazardous routes, with loose rocks, sharp switchbacks, and no handholds.

The southern end of the peninsula is marked by Point Fermin's historic lighthouse which looks west to Catalina Island and east to **Cabrillo Beach** on Los Angeles Harbor. Separated by the 1,000-ft.-long San Pedro breakwater are the two popular beaches at Cabrillo. Surf rolls onto the shore on the ocean side; the harbor's still water laps the sand on the inside. Together they provide safe swimming and windsurf launching. There are picnic facilities, a snack bar, showers, and parking. Cabrillo Marine Aquarium naturalists conduct tidepool tours on the beaches, whale watch boat trips, and interpret plant and animal life in the 32 tanks inside the beach museum.

A favorite waterfront trail starts at Cabrillo Beach and climbs uphill to Point Fermin Park. The handsome Victorian-style lighthouse and observation points in this 37-acre

Doug Propst   LITTLE HARBOR, CATALINA ISLAND

park provide spectacular ocean panoramas. From here the two-mile blufftop walk leads to **Royal Palms**, a state beach popular with surfers. Continuing west, a rocky, pebbled shoreline makes the walking rough, but at low tide the tidepools are worth exploring.

Cabrillo Beach's other interesting walk is out onto the San Pedro breakwater and fishing pier. Atop this long sea wall that ends at Angel's Gate light, the entrance to Los Angeles Harbor, views include whales, dolphins, and seals as well as water traffic. Several dozen feral cats make their homes in the cracks and crannies of the breakwater rocks. A dedicated band of volunteers feeds these wild cats. When new inhabitants arrive they capture them, take them to the vet for immunizations and neutering, and return them to the company of their fellow refugees.

OTHER AREA BEACHES:

Travelers heading south along the coast, from Malibu to Santa Monica will discover three fine south-facing beaches:

Malibu Lagoon State Beach *– This 167-acre beach includes a small brackish lagoon at the mouth of Malibu Creek, as well as Malibu Lagoon Museum, Pier and Surfrider Beach. There are picnic tables, interpretive trails, volleyball, showers, lifeguards. Open sunrise to sunset.*

Las Tunas County Beach*, a narrow, sandy and rocky beach below the bluff. Swimmers and divers beware of sand-holding rusted metal deposits in the water.*

Topanga County Beach *– Narrow, sandy beach (sometimes rocky) with 1 mile of ocean frontage. Popular surfing area near Topanga Creek. Separate parking lot at beach level for vehicles carrying wheelchairs.*

SOUTHERN COAST

M. Burgess, Long Beach Area CVB   NAPLES ISLAND GONDOLIERS

LONG BEACH

Long Beach, eastern arm of the megaport of Los Angeles County, has excellent beaches as well as yacht marinas, tanker and nearby cruise ship terminals, charter boats, harbor tours and the historic ocean liner *Queen Mary*, now a hotel. Seaward of Ocean Boulevard., **Shoreline Aquatic Park's** wide sandy beaches reach 5-½ miles, from the mouth of the Los Angeles River to **Seal Beach** on the Orange County line. Facilities include volleyball courts, concessions, lifeguard stations, and a paved 3-1/2-mile pedestrian/bicycle path. This area has very little surf since the beach lies inside the harbor breakwater. Seafood restaurants, playground equipment, bike and windsurf rentals, picnic tables and sightseer benches make this strand a very inviting locale.

    The Belmont Veterans Memorial Pier has a snack bar, bait and tackle shop, sportfishing boat trips, and whale watch expeditions. **Long Beach Peninsula** features a pedestrian boardwalk, handball and basketball courts. Summer concerts are held at the south end of the peninsula beach. **Alamitos Bay**, also within the Long Beach Breakwater, harbors 2,000 boats, marine suppliers, boat hoists and launches, restaurants, yacht clubs, shops, and a narrow swimming beach. An annual Christmas Parade of lighted boats and floats draws spectators from miles away.

    Naples, a cluster of 3 man-made residential islands inside Alamitos Bay, is a stroller's delight. Italian gondoliers sing to their passengers as they pole through the network of canals, an enchanting sunset scene.

SOUTHERN COAST

Mary Louise Fulton — SURFING AT HUNTINGTON BEACH

ORANGE COUNTY

Between Los Angeles and San Diego counties lies the seashore most noted for its resort activities and ambiance. Tops for surfers is Huntington Beach. For sightseers, it's the artists' colony at **Laguna Beach**; and for boating of every kind, **Newport Beach**. Settled as a resort area in the late 1800s, the county is named for the orange groves that once stretched inland from the sea. Development brought fishing and pleasure piers, warm sandy swimming and surfing beaches, yacht harbors, beach hotels, and vacation cottage colonies.

The **Seal Beach** pier is one of California's longest wooden piers. Deep-sea fishing trips, sportfishing boats and a restaurant are located along the pier, which adjoins a park and beach playground. Travelers can enjoy walkways, a bike path, and frequent aquatic sport festivals. This is a year-round surfing beach.

Between Huntington Harbor and Huntington Beach Pier is 6-mile **Bolsa Chica State Beach** Across the Pacific Coast Highway a 300-acre wetland, Balsa Chica Ecological Reserve, has wildlife viewing areas and access to a loop trail with interpretive signs for identifying endangered birds.

Its 3-mile sandy beach, huge waves, and challenging currents make **Huntington State Beach** the site of international surfing contests. A multi-use paved trail and ramps bring onlookers to the action. The International. Surfing Museum in Huntington Beach exhibits surfing memorabilia, antique boards, and photos.

Mary Louise Fulton — PLAYING ON THE BEACH

To the south, **Newport's** long, sandy beach—narrow at the north end of the peninsula—widens at the Balboa end. Balboa Pavilion is the hub of **Newport Harbor**. The complex offers equipment rentals, fishing licenses, bait and tackle, gift shops, a terminal for Catalina Island excursions and whale watch trips, and a small carnival with rides. A tiny ferry carries passengers and a few cars between the Pavilion and **Balboa Island** within the bay.

Newport Bay and its islands are ideal for strollers. Throughout the area are walkways, benches, picnic facilities, basketball and tennis courts, playgrounds, shops, delis and restaurants. The scene is a colorful tapestry of sails, luxury yachts, children in rowboats and outboards, skimming windsurfers, and sailing classes rounding the race buoys. **China Cove** and **Corona del Mar State Beach**, on the eastern side of the Newport Harbor entrance, have good surfing and swimming beaches. Marine biologists give **Little Coronado del Mar Beach** and **Crystal Cove State Park** high marks for their rocky tidepools and reefs.

Just east of **Dana Point Harbor** is **Doheny State Beach**, a mile-long beach with a 5-acre lawn that has picnic tables, campsites, and fire rings. The water here is rarely without surfers. Offshore is an underwater park for divers. Travelers can pull off the Coast Highway at any of a dozen beaches from Laguna to the San Diego County line. **San Clemente's** palm-studded beach with full-service municipal pier is near California's first mission, San Juan Capistrano.

SOUTHERN COAST

Bob Yarbrough, San Diego CVB   STAIRWAY ACCESS TO THE BEACH

SAN DIEGO COUNTY

Virtually the entire 76-mile coastline of San Diego County is sandy beach backed by steep eroding bluffs. With a long history as the home port of large commercial fishing fleets, **San Diego Bay** is known today for the west coast's largest navy base and as a center for boating of every kind. Military maneuvers and global shipping, as well as complete aquatic recreation—sportfishing, whale watch cruises, beach events, and world-class yacht racing—guarantee a saltwater environment surpassed nowhere in the world.

Secluded beaches and park sites offer escape from the bustle of shore- and water-sports amusements. In this year-round mild climate of almost endless sunshine, summer and winter temperatures average 65–75°F., water temperatures in the mid-60s with warmer swimming in sheltered coves and lagoons.

San Onofre State Beach includes **Trestles Beach**, a favorite with surfers, and **Bluffs Beach** with tent and trailer spaces and hiking trails from campground to beach. **Oceanside's** man-made harbor has small craft berthing with facilities for fishing, sailing instruction, and chartering craft of all kinds. From December to March there are whale watching cruises. The amphitheater hosts a variety of concerts and the 1942-foot long pier makes an excellent strolling and fishing venue. Oceanside's swimming beach and surfing areas are separated from town by a wide, paved, tree-studded bike/pedestrian path.

South from Oceanside are **Carlsbad State Beaches** (North and South), approached by stairways from the blufftop viewing platforms. These sandy and rocky beaches are popular for

San Diego CVB — SUNNING ON THE BEACH

swimming, surfing, diving and fishing. Campsites, services, and equipment rentals are available on the south beach.

Amtrak has 9 daily trains that parallel the coast between Los Angeles and San Diego. For about half of the 2-1/2-hour trip, passengers have an unobstructed view of ocean and shore. Between Oceanside and the Del Mar station the train passes 5 wildlife marshes and inlets. At Del Mar, beach go-ers can be in the surf within minutes of stepping off the train. San Diego's downtown station is only 4 blocks from bay edge, the Broadway Pier and the Maritime Museum.

Between Carlsbad and Del Mar are three state beaches: **Leucadia** (Beacon's Beach), **San Elijo**, and **Cardiff**. They feature good swimming, surfing, skin diving, and surf fishing. San Elijo has blufftop camping facilities. Cardiff adds boat launching, tide pools, and summer lifeguard patrols.

La Jolla is noted for its wide white sand beach. Nearby, brilliantly colored hot air balloons float over **Torrey Pines State Beach**, and the Stephen Birch Aquarium at **Scripps Institution of Oceanography**. A footpath along La Jolla bluffs provides panoramic views of the ocean, beach, and caves created by constant wave action. Look for nesting and resting perches for cormorants and migrating shorebirds.

La Jolla Cove excels in two extremes. Because of mammoth waves that break on the rocky shore, **Boomer Beach** is the choice of expert surfers. However, just to the south is **The Children's Pool**, where a sea wall shields the wave actions and creates a lagoon just right for wading and swimming. Seals and sea lions like this spot too and can crowd both children and adults off the beach. Not to worry, there are others nearby.

James Blank San Diego CVB   BLUFFS ALONG THE COAST

San Diego maps identify over 30 sandy beaches, each with distinct choices. Most popular with the younger crowd are **Pacific Beach** and **Mission Beach**, north of the entrance to Mission Bay. Their action-packed boardwalk, roller coaster and Crystal Pier make this the trendy place to jog, roller skate, bike, shop, and picnic. Family outing locations are the less crowded **La Jolla Shores** beaches. For best scuba diving and snorkeling, go to the clear turquoise waters of **La Jolla Cove** and the **Underwater Marine Reserve**.

The waterways of the 4,600-acre aquatic playground of **Mission Bay** are voted tops by both novice and experienced wind surfers. Catamarans, sailboats, power boats, row boats, and water skis can be rented at bayshore hotels, marinas, and anchorages which offer lessons too. **Sea World**, on the southern end of Mission Bay, is a 150-acre aquarium and theme park with rides, gift shops, snack bars and marine mammal shows.

Greater San Diego is truly a water wonderland. Beach combing, boating, fishing, skin and scuba diving, swimming, whale watching—San Diego has them all. For bayshore spectators there is an endless variety of events—college crew races, kayak and sailboard contests, air and sea exercises from the United States Pacific Fleet and the Naval Air Station, sailing regattas, and opportunities to cruise or sail on historic vessels based at San Diego's docks.

Since its construction in 1854, Point Loma Lighthouse has guided ships into San Diego Bay. On a high promontory

James Aronovsky, Coronado Visitor Info.   BRIDGE TO CORONADO ISLAND

of the **Cabrillo National Monument** peninsula, the lighthouse is telescope-equipped for viewing whale migrations, cruise ships, cargo vessels, and ocean-going yachts. Narrow, sandy beaches are located below **Point Loma** on **Shelter Island**. A bicycle/pedestrian trail runs the length of the "island" to the scenic shoreline of La Playa at the entrance to the yacht harbor.

Across a long, graceful bridge from downtown, the Coronado Peninsula offers superb beaches and promenades on either the still-water shores of **Glorietta Bay** or the open ocean. **Silver Strand State Beach** is a great place for surfing, swimming, clamming, and surf fishing. Bikes can be rented in Coronado for an oceanside ride 5 miles south to **Imperial Beach**.

Near the Mexican border, the **Tijuana River National Estuarine Research Reserve**, a rich habitat of wetlands and dunes for migratory and resident birds and wildlife, is an important educational research center. The estuary staff monitors the growth of bulrushes they've introduced to cleanse occasionally polluted river water. It's a marvelous place to view rare western birds that thrive in these marshes. Guided nature walks leave from the Visitors Center.

Finally, at **Border Field State Park**, near the U.S.-Mexico border, equestrians can gallop their horses along the edge of the surf. This 2-mile stretch of beach is not recommended for swimming.

David Houston   DIVER READY FOR UNDERWATER EXPLORATION

POPULAR UNDERWATER SITES

Aquariums are fascinating, but for a first-hand encounter with the colorful undersea world of Southern California you need a swim suit, snorkel, fins, and mask. Wear a wetsuit in cooler months. For greatest visibility and safety, frequent coves and other protected waters on calm days. Heavy surf raises sand and sediment that clouds the water. From north to south are listed some of the region's best snorkeling spots. Kelp beds attract scuba divers but are omitted here because inexperienced snorkelers can become tangled in the kelp's dense growth.

Always swim close to the rocky outcroppings to view the great variety of plants and creatures living in the warmer, shallow underwater reserve. Enjoy, but remember that coastal law prohibits removing or even moving any plant or animal, no matter how insignificant or how plentiful they might appear.

Malibu. South of Paradise Cove, Point Dume has some good rocky places close to shore, just west of the pier. Early morning and evening are the best times to find a quiet clear sea.

Palos Verdes Peninsula. On the north shore of the peninsula, Malaga Cove, Bluff Cove, and Lunada Bay have extensive underwater colonies. Only Malaga Cove has a paved path down from the bluff; other approaches are steeper and more hazardous. On the peninsula's west shore, Abalone Cove is accessed by a long footpath from the parking lot on Palos Verdes Drive.

Bill Brush   ISTHMUS REEF, CATALINA ISLAND

Santa Catalina Island. Diving shops in Avalon rent snorkeling equipment for enjoyment of the clear, sparkling water just southeast of the passenger boat dock. Children can swim close to shore in shallow water surrounding reefs. Two Harbors Dive and Recreation Center rents equipment for snorkeling and scuba diving and also operates trips to the local dive and snorkeling sites. Excellent shore-side snorkeling areas.

Newport Beach. Just east of Newport Harbor's entrance jetty, sheltering cliffs make good snorkeling off the beaches at Big Corona and Little Corona. Flat, sandy bottoms and rocky reefs characterize both areas. Swim lines and kelp bed barriers protect snorkelers from boat traffic.

At Reef Point, part of **Crystal Cove's** three-mile beach, snorkelers swim with perch, brilliant orange garibaldis, lobsters, and octopus. Access is from a parking lot above. Three coves offer swimming, surfing, tidepooling, and snorkeling in the offshore area, designated an underwater park.

Laguna Beach. Excellent snorkeling locations are tucked under cliffs in a protected ecological preserve. The Rock Pile, Picnic Beach, and Divers Cove are accessible from parking space on Cliff Drive. For a short swim offshore, Woods Cove offers a large rock and reef to be explored. Check at the lifeguard towers for surf conditions that change with wind and tide.

La Jolla. Best-known part of the underwater park is La Jolla Cove. On a calm day, snorkelers are treated to intimate views of a great variety of below-the-surface activity. Patchy reefs and sandy bottom make Marine Street Beach and Windansea Beach ideal for snorkeling.

Lure of the Docks & Piers

More California travelers patronize oceanfront piers and docks, and ramble through busy marinas than bask on its sandy beaches. They walk out on the piers to shop, cast a line for red snapper or halibut, play for prizes in the amusement arcades, eat fish and chips at stand-up counters, or dine by candlelight in gourmet restaurants. Here is a roundup of pleasure piers, some of which already have been mentioned by county.

Crescent City Harbor: lumber docks for freighters, small boat basin, and Citizens' Dock, a 900-foot public wharf. Fish processing plants and a Coast Guard station are here, along with restaurants, diving and marine suppliers, groceries, and fuel.

Eureka: Humboldt Bay: Woodley Island Marina, mooring for commercial and pleasure craft, 1890 Table Bluff Lighthouse, restaurants.

San Francisco Bay and Ocean Piers:

Fort Mason: exhibitions, galleries, music and theatre. Moored at Pier 3 is the *U.S.S. Jeremiah O'Brien*, a World War II Liberty Ship, open to the public.

Fisherman's Wharf: one of the nation's most visited tourist attractions. Sea lions haul out to dry off and pile on top of each other on the docks to the delight of onlookers. Bay views and ocean traffic, dining choices, educational shows, shops, rides, history and nature exhibits, make this cluster of piers a non-stop carnival. Passengers embark from here on ferries to Alcatraz Island, Sausalito, Berkeley, Oakland, and on cruise ships for the Orient and Mexico.

Aquatic Park: 1,850-ft.-long municipal pier with National Maritime Museum, fishing, historic ships, tours, and a bookstore.

Sharp Park Beach and *Pacifica Pier*: 1,100-ft.-long municipal fishing pier, concessions, and bait shop, along Beach Boulevard, Pacifica.

Pillar Point Pier: fishing, boat ramp, charter boats, and food services, on Half Moon Bay in San Mateo County.

Santa Cruz Municipal Wharf: half-mile long car and pedestrian wharf; boat and rental shops, restaurants, fishing, souvenirs.

Capitola Fishing Wharf: boat rentals, bait and tackle shop; wooden stairway from base of pier to the beach.

Seacliff State Beach & Pier: pier leads to 435-foot concrete supply ship, the World War I *Palo Alto*, near Capitola.

Monterey Fisherman's Wharf: fish markets, snack bars, restaurants, boat hoist, shops, galleries, sightseeing cruises,

Santa Barbara CVB   MARINA PIER

the Wharf Theatre, glass-bottomed boat tours. Hundreds of sea lions and seals bark for handouts on the wet, black boulders.

Monterey Coast Guard Pier: launch ramp, fishing and diving area, stairway to San Carlos Beach, access to adjacent Cannery Row immortalized by John Steinbeck.

Morro Bay's T-Piers: fishing and commercial boat docking, restaurant, bait and tackle shop, public showers. Two U.S. Coast Guard cutters berth at North T-Pier, usually open for tours.

Port San Luis Pier and Beach: 1,320-ft.-long pier, lit all night. Gas and diesel fuel dock, trailer boat hoist, Avila Beach access. Disabled may drive onto pier. South of San Luis Obispo.

Pismo Beach Pier: 1,250-ft.-long pier in the middle of town. Concession stand, fishing equipment rentals, nearby shops and restaurants. Surfing allowed on south side of pier.

Gaviota Fishing Pier: Santa Barbara County in Gaviota State Beach, there is a boat launch, bait and tackle shop.

Gioleta Beach Pier: Excellent fishing pier equipped with a boat-hoist, hosted by Santa Barbara County Parks Department.

Stearns Wharf (Santa Barbara): originally constructed in 1872 as a seaport landing for cargo, passenger, and fishing ships. Restored wharf attractions: restaurants, stores, a seafood market, the Sea Center with exhibits on the marine resources of the ocean environment of Channel Islands National Park that includes the adjacent islands of Anacapa, Santa Cruz, Santa Rosa, San Miguel and Santa Barbara. Adjacent *Santa Barbara Harbor Marina* includes 1,000 docked yachts, sportfishing excursions, and marine specialty shops.

Ventura Pier: Originally built in 1872 the Ventura Pier has a reasonable claim as.the longest wooden pier in California. Snack bar, bait shop, large restaurant; 30 interpretive panels describe local history and marine environment. The pier is part of *San Buenaventura State Beach..*

Malibu Pier: 700-ft. wooden pier built 1903, fishing licenses, bait & tackle, sportfishing boats, restaurant; part of *Malibu Lagoon State Beach..*

Santa Monica Municipal Pier: world-famous carrousel, amusement arcades, restaurants, food concessions, shops, boating and pier fishing. Seasonal musical, theatrical or circus performances. Pier divides Santa Monica's wide, sandy north and south beaches.

Marina del Rey (Los Angeles): world's largest artificial boat harbor. Though not anchored by a pier, Marina is a small city of high rises, docks, harborside walks, and saltwater activities. Endless menu of waterside entertainments in this huge anchorage. Eight separate channels are home to 6,200 private pleasure craft, seven yacht clubs, sailing schools, boat rentals, hotels, shops, and restaurants of every size, price and cuisine.

Manhattan Beach Municipal Pier: 900 feet long, the pier is located at the foot of Manhattan Beach Boulevard.. Bike racks, volley ball courts, fishing, outdoor showers, dressing and restrooms. Located at the end of the pier is the Roundhouse Marine Studies Lab and Aquarium with an extensive collection of marine life.

Hermosa Beach Pier: extends from the broad beach's South Bay Bicycle Promenade and the Esplanade. Both shoppers and fishermen use pier, along with travelers watching surfing, diving and paddling competitions.

Redondo Beach Piers (on King Harbor seashore):

Sportfishing Pier: bait and tackle shop, equipment sales and rentals, charters, coffee shop, snack bar and whale-watching cruises.

Municipal Pier: an array of dining establishments, fish markets, kite shop, concerts, boutiques; large amusement arcade on lower garage level.

Monstad Pier: One of the best fishing spots in Southern California. Bait and tackle shop, restaurants, the fishing platform is at the seaward end.

E. Baxter, Long Beach Area CVB　　　SHORELINE PARK, QUEEN MARY

Cabrillo Fishing Pier (San Pedro): 1000-ft.-long breakwater; no shops but adjacent to Cabrillo Aquarium and Museum. In Los Angeles Harbor.

Queen Mary Seaport (Long Beach): Aboard and alongside the retired superliner, now a luxury hotel and attraction, are gift shops and restaurants.

Belmont Pier (Long Beach): 1,620-ft.-long T-shaped pleasure pier, at the foot of 39th Place.

The Pleasure Pier (Avalon Bay, Santa Catalina Island): concessions, boat hoist, diving supplies for sale or rent, fishing licenses. Glass-bottomed boats explore Underwater Gardens.

Two Harbors Pier (Isthmus Cove, Santa Catalina): concessions, diving supplies and rental, scuba diving trips, boat trips, and harbor cruises.

Seal Beach Pier: city-owned , sportfishing boats offer half- and full-day deep-sea excursions. Access from pier to grassy park and playground on the sand.

Huntington Beach Pier: 1,853-ft.-long pier re-built from the 1914 original; floodlit at night for fishing and surfing.

Newport Beach Pier: surfing, fishing, fish-cleaning sinks. The Newport Dory Fishing Fleet returns around 8:00 am on the north side of the pier to sell catch on the beach. Full service restaurant.

James Blank, San Diego CVB CHILDREN'S POOL BEACH

Balboa Beach and Pier (Newport Harbor): terminal for Catalina Island tours, harbor cruises, whalewatch boats and charters, sportfishing and marine recreation.

Aliso Beach Pier: 620 feet long, snack bar, bait and tackle shop. Access by pedestrian tunnel from east side of Pacific Coast Hwy.

San Clemente Municipal Pier: Food concessions, fish cleaning sinks, bait and tackle, beach with picnic facilities, outdoor showers.

Oceanside Pier: municipal pier with bait and tackle shop, restaurant, and life guard station. Wheelchair-accessible tram runs from pier gate to the end. Strand Pier Plaza at base of pier has amphitheatre and community center.

Ellen Browning Scripps Memorial Pier (La Jolla): 1,090-ft.-long research facility of the Scripps Institution of Oceanography and Shoreline-Underwater Reserve.

Ocean Beach Municipal Pier (San Diego): South of Mission Bay complex. Food concessions, shops, parking, stairs lead to the sandy beach and paved pedestrian/bicycle path.

San Diego City Piers:

  Broadway Pier: embarkation point for the Coronado-San Diego Ferry, a great way to view San Diego Bay and visit Coronado Island's Ferry Landing Marketplace.

  Navy Pier: museum home of the aircraft carrier Midway.

  Embarcadero Fishing Pier: next to Seaport Village Shopping Center on Harbor Drive.

Beverly Ditmars — GULLS & PELICANS ON MALIBU BEACH

PACIFIC FLYWAY

During spring and fall, the coastline is frequented by a variety of migrating birds. California's coastal wetlands provide food and resting areas for thousands of these travelers.

Shorebirds and waterfowl like willets, pintail and canvasback ducks, great blue herons, egrets, avocets, plovers and little sanderlings, visit marshes, bays, and coastlines on their flights south from Canada and Alaska or north from Mexico and Central America. These birds feed primarily on marine invertebrates. Dredging and filling around bays, and intrusion by sightseers, have reduced or eliminated large areas of eelgrass habitats of these invertebrates.

Seabirds spend most of their time flying, feeding at sea, or resting on the open ocean. Unlike oceanbirds such as sheerwaters, albatross and Arctic terns that feed and rest miles from land, shorebirds such as cormorants, grebes, loons, pelicans and scoters feed in shallow water and can be sighted from beaches, cliffs, and intertidal areas. The *Easy Field Guide to Common Sea & Shore Birds of California* is a good take-along for their identification.

Marine life is vulnerable to oil spills, pesticides and overfishing which in turn can cause a decline in bird populations dependent upon fish.

Amanda Fessler   LA JOLLA COVE

FAIR & FESTIVAL CALENDAR

Along the shore, special outdoor events are staged for nearly every week of the year, culminating in year-end holiday celebrations in harbor and bay.

JANUARY:

January is prime to watch the California Gray Whale migration as thousands move south along the state's 840 mile coast. Gray whales migrate close to shore so most any pier or bluff will give you a good view. Whale Watching Cruises are available. Prime locations to spot whales are:

Big Sur	Newport Beach	San Diego
Dana Point	Point Fermin	Santa Barbara
Humbolt Bay	Redondo Beach	Santa Cruz
Monterey Bay		Ventura

Huntington Beach: New Year Day Pier Plunge

La Jolla: New Year Day Polar Bear Plunge

Santa Monica: New Year Day Santa Monica Pier Resolution Festival

Venice Beach: Penguin Swim Club New Year's Dive

Half Moon Bay: Mavericks surfing competition

FEBRUARY:

Whale watching continues

    Huntington Beach: Kite flying and design competition
    Santa Cruz Beach Boardwalk: Clam Chowder Festival
    Dana Point: Whale festival
    Long Beach: Regatta of Sailing Vessels
    Pismo Beach: Mardi Gras Jazz Festival

MARCH:

Whale watching continues all along the coast.

March through August Grunion spawn at night on many beaches in Southern California. During the Open Seasons, Grunion are taken by using your hands, no holes may be dug in the beach to entrap them. A fishing license is required for persons over 16. Cabrillo State Beach in San Pedro offers a Grunion Program on several nights during the season.

> **Dana Point**: Whale festival

APRIL:

Closed Season for Grunion

> **Bodega Bay**: Fisherman's Festival. Boat parade and blessing of the fleet.

MAY:

Closed Season for Grunion

> **Huntington Beach:** Duck-a-thon
>
> **Sunset Beach**: Art Festival
>
> **Del Mar**: National Horse Show "where the turf meets the surf."

JUNE:

Open Season for Grunion

> **Huntington Beach**: Pier Swim
>
> **Santa Cruz**: Pro-Am Beach Soccer Tournament
>
> **Santa Barbara**: Summer Solstice Festival
>
> **Newport Beach**: Newport Heritage Regatta

JULY:

Open Season for Grunion

Fourth of July Fireworks from Beaches and Piers are a guaranteed delight.

Venues with consistently spectacular fireworks displays include:

Avalon	Huntington Beach	Oxnard
Cabrillo Beach	Chula Vista	Long Beach
Coronado	Newport Beach	Pismo Beach
	San Francisco	

LaJolla: Concerts by the Sea every Sunday in Scripts Park at LaJolla Cove

Huntington Beach: US Open Beach Games

San Clemente: Ocean Festival

Imperial Beach: US Open Sandcastle Competition

Berkeley Marina: Professional kite fliers as well as family fun

Santa Barbara: Semana Nautica Summer Sports Festival

AUGUST:

Open Season for Grunion

Channel Islands Harbor: McNish Classic Yacht Race

San Diego: World Body Surfing Championships

Long Beach: Capture the Wind Kite Festival

Huntington Beach: Boardfest events for surf, skate and snow boards

SEPTEMBER:
- **Pacifica**: Pacific Coast Fog Fest
- **San Luis Obispo**: Morro Bay Triathlon
- **Newport Beach**: Sailing Regatta and windsurfing competition
- **Corona Del Mar**: Sandcastle Contest
- **Dana Point**: Tall Ships Festival and Sea Chantey Concert

OCTOBER:
- **San Francisco**: Blessing of the Fleet
- **Monterey**: Monarch Butterfly Festival
- **Pismo Beach**: Clam Festival
- **Natural Bridge State Beach**: Celebration of the return of the Monarch Butterfly
- **Catalina Island**: JazzTrax Festival
- **Santa Cruz**: Halloween on the Wharf

NOVEMBER:

DECEMBER:
- **Channel Islands Harbor:** Parade of Lights
- **Huntington Beach:** Cruise of Lights
- **Newport Harbor**: Holiday Boat Parade "deck the hulls"
- **San Diego Bay:** Parade of Lights

BEACH ETIQUETTE

On some California Beaches, there are ordinances prohibiting smoking and alcoholic beverages. Horses and dogs are banned on some, while others welcome them. Clothing optional beaches are scattered along the coast except in Los Angeles County where public nudity is against the law. At clothing optional sites, laws or protocols ban lewd activity, gawking and photography. Some exclusions and dispensations are in effect continuously, others for specified hours. Check with the local authorities before you leave your bathing suit behind, bring your pet or pick up a six-pack.

STATE BEACH ACTIVITIES & FACILITIES

California State Parks Department administers the State Beaches. Their website at www.parks.ca.gov contains activity and facility information for all. District Offices manage the Beaches in their region:

Eureka	North Coast Redwood District	(707) 445-6547
Mendocino	Mendocino District	(707) 937-5804
Petaluma	Marin District	(707) 769-5665
Felton	Santa Cruz District	(831) 335-6318
Monterey	Monterey District	(831) 649-2836
San Simeon	San Luis Obispo Coast District	(805) 927-2065
Ventura	Channel Coast District	(805) 585-1850
Calabasas	Angeles District	(818) 880-0350
San Clemente	Orange Coast District	(949) 492-0802
San Diego	San Diego Coast District	(619) 688-3260